Big Birdie

by Patricia Gould

Printed and bound in the United States of America
First printing • ISBN # 978-0-9998884-0-7
Copyright © 2018

Big Birdie

by Patricia Gould

FOR ORDER INFORMATION VISIT
www.scottpublishingcompany.com

PayPal
MasterCard VISA AMERICAN EXPRESS DISCOVER NETWORK

SCOTT COMPANY PUBLISHING
P.O. Box 9707 • Kalispell, MT 59904
Toll Free: 1-800-628-0212
Fax: 1-406-756-0098
www.scottpublishingcompany.com

This book is dedicated to my elders, who nurtured the confidence in me, even as a small child, to achieve my dreams. Courage and selflessness were required for an unwavering faith in my abilities. Many would think it unwise to allow a small child fascinated with horses so much freedom with such large animals. I grew up in a loving family who had the intuition and wisdom to know it was more foolhardy to deny me the one thing I yearned to attain. The destiny I envisioned was to ride a magnificent horse.

Chapter 1
More than Turnips

Mom loved turnips. That was the reason for our drive to Griff's farm that morning. I remember it so vividly, even now, over 50 years later. Earlier in the week, at O'Bannon's Feed store, a gathering place where local rural residents of my tiny, home town up-dated each other on current events. Griff was boasting of his turnip patch and welcomed anyone who liked or needed turnips to come on out and help themselves.

Arthur McGriff, known to most everyone as Griff, was an elderly bachelor with a 40-acre farm. It was just a few miles east of ours. The unique aspect regarding Griff, considering it was now the early 1960's, was that he still farmed with a team of draft horses.

I don't recall details of our trip or our arrival, but I'll never forget what happened next. After catching up on the latest neighborhood news with Mom, he was delighted to learn we were there for turnips. As we followed him

to the barn, he gestured to the hollow beyond. His turnip patch was there. He had one thing to do first, he explained. As he opened the barn door, you could see his winter storage of turnips and onions in bundles, tied with twine, hanging everywhere from the barn rafters. Turnips were not why this morning became forever so memorable to me. From inside the barn the soft, staccato nickering of three enormous horses welcomed us with endearing resonance in their voices beckoning, "Come closer". The trio stirring within their stalls sent tremors through the wood plank flooring. They chorused joyous anticipation for companionship from their visitors.

From three stall doors, the horses towered above us along the barn aisle. As I went from each velvety nose, breathing and snorting plumed from their nostrils in the chilly October morning air. Griff, with his slight, elderly frame had to reach upwards to grasp each halter as he introduced his Percherons.

We first met Barney, standing at attention with his head held high. Barney was well over 18 hands high, lean and powerful. He was a fiery crimson bay horse. His coppery body was accented with a bold, white blaze flowing down his face from his forehead to his nose and a long, black mane and tail. His fetlocks were silky feathers of black hair fluttering around his hooves as he stepped about in his stall.

Billy was in the next stall. Though not as tall as Barney, he displayed a broad, muscular chest and hindquarters, giving him the classic look of a draft horse. His black coat glistened into iridescent shades of blue and violet.

At the end of the barn aisle, in a corner stall stood Birdie, who had not stopped softly nickering until she also had her pats and scratches. Aside from her calmer, docile demeanor, she was a carbon copy of Billy with the same white star on her forehead and one white sock. I marveled at the size of their hooves, easily as big as dinner plates.

The pride and affection was evident in his voice as Griff explained to us that Billy was Birdie's colt and now, a 5-year-old, big and strong enough to work alongside his bigger, 7-year-old gelding, Barney. Birdie was now 12. She had worked hard for him all those years and he wanted the rest of her days to be carefree. No more plows or hard work for Birdie. His knowledge and skill to train these huge animals instantly won my respect and admiration. This man obviously loved his horses.

As if in anticipation of our unspoken request, he plucked a bridle from its' nail on the wall and insisted these three little girls should have a ride. With the three of us perched upon Birdie's solid, broad bareback, he led the mare out of the barn and down to the turnip patch.

It didn't take long for the five of us to pull enough turnips to fill Mom's boxes. During the entire time my sisters and I persistently tried to convince Griff to sell Birdie. To our amazement, he finally answered, yes. He was willing to sell her to someone who would provide her a good home and the retirement she deserved. We immediately began pestering Mom to buy her for us. To have this giant of a horse for our very own was beyond my wildest imagination!

You must have sympathy for Mom. It was three against one. She didn't stand a chance. Apparently I was born a stubborn character. Family members who knew me in my early childhood, well before my recollection of events, fill in the blanks like this. They say, at a very young age, when determined to get my way, I would hold my breath until I turned blue. During one tantrum, (I did not want to stop "playing" Grandma's piano.), not only did I turn blue, I blacked out, toppling from the piano bench. Mom, in her patient wisdom, calmly made a trip to the kitchen for a glass of water. When she returned, she splashed water on my face to revive me. That may have discouraged me from holding my breath as a means of getting my way, but not my determination to pursue my goals.

As far back as I can recall, I've had a fascination with all creatures; deer, rabbits, skunks, goats, horses, lizards, turtles, birds and many others. I was 5 years old when I heard for the first time, the expression, "If you can salt a bird's tail, you can capture it because it would be unable to fly away." Daunted by the reality of my own inability to get close enough to salt a bird's tail, (Maybe I had tried.) I rationalized a new solution.

My ingenious plan was to salt all the eggs and baby birds I could locate still in their nests. Later, when I encountered those same birds, I could magically catch them. For an entire afternoon I salted every nest I could find throughout the neighborhood. At suppertime, my explanation for misplacing Mom's prized Tupperware salt shaker did not get me out of trouble completely. I was sent out to search, unsuccessfully, for it for the remainder of the day.

Surely an inkling of my inescapable passion for horses has become apparent. Many of you may possess that same tendency and always will. I have read and reread every Walter Farley novel in "The Black Stallion" saga. How I yearned to be Alec Ramsey, swept up in his adventures as fate thrust his path into that world of noble Arabian horses. Someday I hoped to witness the annual, true-life round-up of the legendary ponies of Chincoteague. I had a collection of paperback books telling the stories of Misty, Star and all the other island ponies offered from my school's many Scholastic book fairs. I hoped to never experience the anguish of Jody in Steinbeck's, "The Red Pony". I regretted not living in the days of Scarlett O'Hara and riding the elegant saddle horses bred on the plantations of the old south. With the chance of having a horse, a real horse, I was relentless in my attempts to persuade Mom to say yes.

Finally she agreed to discuss this with Daddy. Knowing this would be a difficult hurdle to overcome, we were not surprised that he was against the idea of such a large horse for his young daughters. He also argued that the past few years had been a struggle starting a dairy farm. Money was scarce and an animal that size would be expensive to feed. But, with Mom now in our corner, he was outnumbered four to one. We, throughout the next year, secretly put a plan in motion to save the money to buy Birdie anyway.

Any spare change, birthday money and chore money was tucked away in our money jar. Finally, just before Thanksgiving, we had enough to buy our horse. Daddy still didn't know.

Chapter 2
Daddy's Big Surprise

Until I became a parent myself, it was impossible to comprehend how tirelessly my dad had worked to support his family. There were times he worked as many as three different jobs at one time. From sun-up until late at night, he never stopped. During this time, between milking and farming much of the day, he drove a 40-something-mile country school bus route. Many nights he would moonlight as a mechanic at the Phillips 66 service station in town. Other nights were spent transporting sports teams and school clubs to out-of-town competitions in sometimes brutal Missouri winter weather.

His experiences with the high school athletes and coaches sparked him to join our town's other frequent fans in the bleachers at many of the local games. Our entire family especially enjoyed traveling the 6 mile trip to town to become extra cheerleaders at intense games for championships and those against longtime rivals.

His busy schedule made it fairly simple for Mom to devise a covert plan to get Birdie to her new home. Our farm truck was a reliable Ford pick-up with stock racks to haul cattle, but an 1800-pound horse was more than it could manage. Her plan was genius. On the day Griff was expecting her to come for Birdie, she waited for Daddy to leave for work. He would not return home until after his night-shift at the gas station. When he had left for town that afternoon, she telephoned our close neighbor, Mollie, already aware of our scheme, for a prearranged shuttle ride to Griff's farm.

My mom had very limited experience with horses. As a young girl, she sometimes helped her dad with the plowing on their Ozark's farm after the depression. My granddad established a truck patch on a few acres atop the same hill I have set my roots, hopefully, for the last time. Those roots have clawed down into those rocks for the last 18 years. Recently I realized my residency at this address surpasses, by many years, the time I have lived in any of my other homes.

They could not afford a horse of their own. Fortunately Grandpa could borrow a neighbor's horse when he needed one. Apparently this mare was a particularly stubborn creature which required two handlers to coax her to stay on task. My mom would lead the horse forward with the bridle while my grandad drove the plow. Whenever this story is retold, the anecdotal ending is, "The mare's name was Nell, but it should have been Hell." In spite of her longstanding mistrust of horses instilled in her so many years ago by cantankerous old Nell, Mom's intent was to ride Birdie home.

As part of the transaction, Griff included a bridle with the horse. With a boost from Griff onto Birdie's bareback, Mom bravely began her journey home. In the beginning their trip went smoothly, but the farther Birdie got from her old home, the more anxious she became. With halfway yet to go, Birdie became determined to turn back and began to balk. Mom's only solution to this dilemma was to get off and continue on by leading her. Later, after Birdie had calmed down, it was impossible for Mom to get back on her alone, leaving her no choice but to lead the mare the remaining distance home. It would be another 40 years before she challenged the sport of horseback riding again.

At the age of 67, she expressed the desire to ride horses with my children and I. We were avid riders. Our recreation time together included trailriding throughout parks in Georgia, Tennessee, Arkansas and Missouri. With Mom's sudden change of heart, our vacations became camping out at horse parks with three generations riding together, mom, daughter and grandkids. She qualified and won "Oldest Woman Rider Award" after riding the entire 25+ miles in a local charity 2-day trail ride. Curiosity once forced me to ask why she had decided, after so many years, to start riding now. Her reply was "If you can't beat 'em, you might as well join 'em."

Looking back, it became clear that her cousin, Betty, was an important influence in Mom's decision to ride with us. Earlier that same summer, cousins from Olympia, Washington, Betty and Alice, were our guests for a while during their vacation. One day, during their stay, while making plans to ride horses, I, almost in jest, invited Betty to join us. She was 76. When reminiscing earlier in the day, she seemed wistful and commented it had been 52 years since she had ridden a horse. With little persuasion, she gratuitously accepted the invitation. We solemnly promised to only walk the horses as she requested. If her intention was to shock everyone there that day, she had succeeded.

Later that day, with the horses saddled and everyone onboard, including Betty, we rode off, keeping the horses at an easy pace. We travelled 2 miles or so before turning back towards home. To our surprise, Betty, and Angel, our perfect horse for any rider, passed us by, leaving us behind in their dust. Betty, totally in control, never reined Angel in to slow her from her perky foxtrot for most of the trip back. When asked about her ride, she assured me the afternoon had been a "hoot!"

Soon after Mom suddenly developed an interest in riding Angel. If Betty could ride her, so could she! But, now back to my story. I do go off on a tangent now and then.

Mom did manage to get Birdie home before Daddy returned from his last job for that day. Birdie was put up in a stall in our big red barn for the night. No one breathed a word of the day's events to him. Thanks to Mom, mission accomplished.

The next morning, as he did everyday, my dad walked from the farmhouse with gleaming stainless steel milk buckets sloshing with steamy hot water in each hand, to begin milking cows. As he went through the gate, Birdie popped her head out of her stall and boldly whinnied to him, no doubt demanding breakfast. He paused long enough to glance in her direction before continuing on to the milk barn.

Shortly after, Mom joined him to help with the milking. The entire time, their conversation not once included Birdie. Only after the milking was finished did he say he guessed he would have to find out just how gentle this horse really was.

He never spoke of riding horses, even as a boy. He had helped his granddad, Pop, as he called him, to farm with his team of horses, but was quick to add he preferred his bike over horses as his transportation back then. But that day, he rode Birdie. He had to maneuver her next to the corral fence to climb on her back. He directed her to walk, trot and whoa. Together they went numerous trips around our circle driveway, now and then, switching to circle in the opposite direction. Satisfied that she would be a safe, gentle horse for his daughters to ride, he returned her to her stall.

Though he had been against buying Birdie, he knew

how much she meant to us. I'm sure Mom stood firm on our side, making him realize how long and hard we had slaved to earn $125 to purchase our horse. He knew very well how much an animal that enormous would eat, but his big heart won over his better judgment. We could keep her, but he made it clear that it would be our responsibility to care for her.

Chapter 3
So You Wanna Be a Cowgirl?

For a 9-year-old girl, dreaming of her own horse for as long as she could remember, that dream had now at last, come true. Sure, Birdie was to be shared with my sisters but they were never as enthusiastic as I about riding or caring for horses.

Every summer, once school vacation had officially arrived, all the grandkids were sent to stay the entire summer in southern Missouri with Grandma and Grandpa Berger. Their farm was located so far from any city or town that our isolation as small children was like stepping back into another era. Grandma refused to ever learn to drive an automobile and with Grandpa's job in Kansas City, over 200

GRANDPA

GRANDMA

miles away, she often existed more like a hermit. But her summers were kept busy with a big, rambling farmhouse full of grandchildren.

During my last few summers spent in the Ozarks, her brood, myself and sisters and all my first cousins, had grown to 9 kids ranging from the ages of 10 through 4. By then Grandpa had retired, but Grandma was in charge and she ran a tight ship. Each child was expected to pitch in with everyday tasks, especially at mealtime. Mondays were laundry day, when all the bed linens would stripped from the 6 or so beds in the house. Everything would be washed in her wringer-washing machine and hung on the outdoor clothes line. Before the end of the day, when the clothes were dry, they would be pulled down from the line, folded and gathered into several laundry baskets. The beds would be remade. The remainder of the newly-laundered items returned to their designated drawer or shelf. Other days were kept busy weeding or watering the garden.

Another chore we were required to do was mow their yard. For many years, I remember using an ancient push-type blade mower. Fortunately the yard was not a large area and often we had help of the four-legged kind. Two, in particular, I remember were young calves we named Jack and Jill. We played together constantly in the yard. Jack and Jill became accustom to their smaller playmates, even allowing us to ride them bareback. They had become yard pets out of necessity.

Grandma always had a milkcow to supply milk for the farm. Each child learned to milk the cows, as well. With practice, efficiency improves. It also helps to not be intimidated, but cautious, of the large cows. At the time Molly and Jet, Jack and Jill's mothers, became milkcows, Grandma and Grandpa were away visiting relatives in Montana. Mom volunteered to stay at their farm to care for the livestock, which included milking Blanchie, the long-time, gentle family milkcow. Blanchie was due to have a calf within weeks. Temporarily retiring the very pregnant cow for maternity leave, Mom chose two cows from the beef herd to milk instead. I suppose you could call her a "cow whisperer" because she managed to tame and milk those wild range cows. The calves were kept in the yard, away from their mothers much of the time, thus sharing the limited supply of milk with the family.

I cannot begin to guess how many gallons of wild raspberries and blackberries we picked during those many summers. In late June the multitude of wild raspberry vines found us challenging their thorns, armed with berry-picking baskets, wide-brimmed staw hats and a dousing of insect repellant to give us a fighting chance against the ticks and chiggars. By the Fourth of July, raspberry picking was over and the blackberries were beginning to ripen. Once again for several weeks we battled the brambles, the heat and bug bites. But the bounty was always worth it. As each basket of fresh berries was delivered to the house, Grandma would wash and pack them into containers to store in the freezer, destined for future cobblers and jams thoughout the next year.

One favorite concoction Grandma was famous for was a recipe she called buckskin jelly. The blackberries and sugar were slowly simmered until the juice and sugar thickened. The end results were tiny Mason jars of dark purple caramelized spread that had the hint of a taste and aroma similar to black strap molasses.

The berry patches are fewer today but I usually manage to stock my freezer with ample berries also destined for several upcoming holiday cobblers and jars of jam.

In late fall, the Ozark's cash crop is black walnuts. Many even call them our "Black Gold". During Thanksgiving vacation, most of us would gather the nuts in 5-gallon buckets throughout the property. Through the many years Grandpa had cleared timber for pasture, but left groves of walnut trees standing, insuring walnut harvests now and for future generations.

Most of the harvest is sold locally to Hammond's, a local company that processes the harvest in various ways. The black, tarry hulls, once removed are sold as fertilizer. The rock-hard shells become abrasives to clean machinery such as jet engines. The nuts become available after harvest in local retail stores. Over the years, Hammond's has expanded their business to include their own shops selling baked goods and candies made with black walnuts. They are still a thriving company and offer more cash per hundred pounds of unhulled walnuts than in the past.

This income keeps many country folks shaking trees and, bucket by bucket, loading pick-up trucks of the "Black Gold" to sell at nearby hulling stations.

Some of the harvest is always kept as a personal supply of nuts for the up-coming year. With a ballpeen hammer, we sat on the concrete slab steps of the wellhouse and cracked walnuts. If the weather was cold or rainy, we cracked our nuts on the cement fireplace hearth indoors. Over the years, small indentations had been worn into the cememt, perfectly cupping the nuts as we hammered them open. Everyone then worked tirelessly to sort the nuts from the shells. Using a metal nutpick, we would extract any pieces lodged within the tiny catacombs of the shell. Over the years, creative recipes using black walnuts have become neverending.

One pasttime every grandkid enjoyed, I truly believe, had to be fishing. We fished often those many summers at Grandpa's stocked pond. It couldn't have been located more than 100 yards from his backdoor. Back then, before someone put catfish in this pond, we would catch a few nice fish. Bass, crappie and bluegill were what we would bring back to the house. On an old, scarred wooden cutting board, we had been taught to clean and scale our fish. Grandma would pan fry them, even the tiny ones, for the next meal. At mealtime we would relive our time at the pond, strongly debating who caught the biggest fish or the most. Our counts always included the ones you caught but threw back because they needed to grow just a little.

One particular fishing afternoon I remember well. Several of the grandkids were fishing. On this day, our Uncle Sever joined our group. Lordy, were we catching the fish that day! With more than a dozen nice fish on our stringer, colorful, trophy-deserving bluegill and several large bass, that day was shaping up to end in a fantastic fish fry feast. In a few short minutes, our feast was not going to happen.

While fishing at a pond, you constantly move along the bank to find the best place where the fish are biting. If someone gets lucky in a particular spot, everyone zones in on that area. At one point, I settled in to fish just next to our stringer of fish. My uncle had secured the chain to a sassafras sapling growing at the edge of the pond. Each time we caught a keeper fish, we would pull the stringer to shore, add the new fish, then throw the entire catch back into the water still tethered to the tree.

Suddenly the tree began to bow as the stringer of fish frantically tugged at it. The water was shallow. I could see most of our fish swimming just under the water. The water became churned and muddy. As the fish swirled around and upside down, one, long golden belly drew my attention. The underbelly of a bluegill is similarly golden. Nowhere would anyone catch a bluegill this size. Being curious, I pulled the heavy chain of fish out of the water. Entangled around the catch, writhing and striking, was an enormous cottonmouth snake. I screamed, dropped everything back into the pond and ran.

My uncle, after struggling through the underbrush from the other side of the pond, was beside me. After calming me down, he was able to understand what I had witnessed, why I was terrified. He then hoisted the monstrosity out of the water. The snake was still clinging and attacking. Unlike me, he was brave enough to toss the stringer onto the pond bank and find something to kill the snake. With our fish back in the water, we returned to our poles to fish again a short time longer, unsucessfully, while one by one our feast floated to the surface, the unlucky victims of the venomous snake.

Unlike the many times we had fished in the Ozarks, we attempted hunting bullfrogs only once. The adults often hunted frogs. The reward of froglegs for supper was our motivation to try it on our own. That venture unfolded the last summer I spent with my grandparents. Now older, we were more daring in our attempts to stay entertained.

We set out one warm night, the countryside illuminated by a full moon. Our equiptment consisted of fishing poles with tags of stop-sign-red cloth pierced and threaded onto the hooks, a flashlight and a sack. The reasoning for red rags for bait was our longstanding belief that big bullfrogs, like real bulls, attacked red objects. We braved the darkened pondbank, listening and searching for the biggest frogs.

While hypnotizing our prey with the flashlight beamed

directly at a frog, another child would edge close enough to dangle the cloth-draped hook into its' face. The sport is to snag the frog under its' chin before it sprang with a startling squeek and a splash several yards away. On some occasions, we would lose our red scraps of cloth during the struggle. When we ran out of "bait", we improvised with plump, unripe, so-still-red blackberries conveniently growing nearby.

After circling the pond, the frog population in that hunting zone became wary and impossible to catch. Giving up, our hunting party trekked up the hill with poles, flashlight and our sack of frogs to the next pond. This pond yielded several additional large frogs to our catch. Crossing the open field toward home our celebrated reward for bravely stalking into the late-night countryside quickly turned to dismay. Our frogs had escaped. Their shimmering, silvery images, clearly visible in the mooonlit field, were hopping frantically away in all directions. Our novice mistake, and later humiliation, was trusting a brown paper grocery bag to safely contain our fine mess of fat, wet frogs.

Now and then, we were Grandpa's crew. We would join him and his chainsaw and axe in the timbered portions of his property. As he felled and sawed the tree, then chopped the logs into firewood, our job was to load it onto his wagon. It was on one of those excursions that Grandpa allowed me to drive his tractor. I was sitting on his lap, of course. That summer I was 8 years old.

The loads of firewood were then stacked on the porch to burn in their fireplace for winter heat and for Grandma's ornate, cast-iron Daisy wood cookstove which she still used year-round.

The Ozarks have an abundance of natural resourses. We utilized many of them, building on our previous generations' knowledge and methods. Rocks were plentiful, a hindrance in the wrong place but useful with a little hard work and ingenuity. Teamwork between the young and old cleared the pastures of wagonloads of the loose and imbedded stones, one area at a time. In time, with erosion and the constant hoof traffic from the cattle, another sweep of gathering rocks would be necessary. The old folk saying is that the Ozarks hills never run out of rocks. They just grow more.

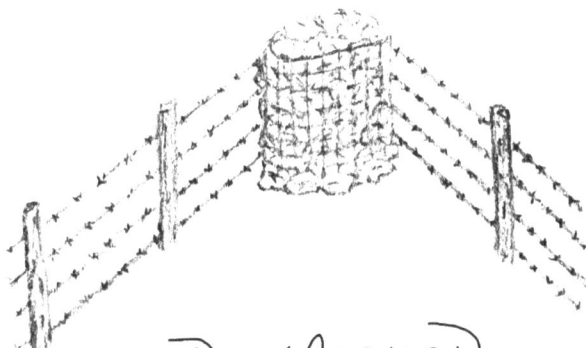

ROCK CORNER POST

The rocks were then used as filler in foundations for the many barns and sheds Grandpa constantly constructed. This helped to minimize the cost of expensive concrete. For fences, the rocks were stacked in large rings of woven wire to serve as corner posts to support miles and miles of fencing. Most of these rock pillars still dot the countryside stamping the patchwork boundaries of the property.

We were even taught the craft of stuccoing. This

masonary technique applies a mortar-like layer to the wooden siding of buildings. This preserves the native oak boards far superior to painting them. After nailing chicken wire to the entire, exposed sides of a building, a mix of sand, mortar and water are blended together with a shovel in his wheelbarrow. The mix is trowled onto the wire. When dry and cured, the stucco encased the building in a tough, gritty shell. With the exception of the old outhouse, those buildings still stand today.

Many might think the we were more like slave labor to our grandparents, but that was not the case at all. Each day a specific chore was designated for us to complete. When finished, the rest of the day was ours to spend as we pleased in exploring the vast surrounding outdoors, building forts or seeking new fantastic adventures inspired through our imaginations. I feel fortunate, richer for these unique experiences. It instilled in me a strong work ethic, an important key for success as an adult.

More importantly, my grandparents and older relatives created a benign and carefree environment where we thrived. One wise word of advice my grandmother constantly encouraged me to follow. She insisted that the young should cherish and appreciate the energy and freedom of childhood. Soon enough you will grow up to assume the responsibilities now shouldered by the adults who surround you with love and protection. I have relayed her message to my children and will again someday to my grandchildren.

Grandpa was the first the recognize the obvious symptoms of horse fever in his young granddaughters during an afternoon at Fairyland Park, an amusement park in Kansas City. Apparently, we had been so delighted with the pony rides that he bought two ponies from the park and had them shipped to his farm. For several years those Shetland ponies whetted our appetite for exploring the world of horses. The older pony we named Sandy because of his golden color. With a large, white patch resembling a star on his forhead, the smaller pony, we called Starry. Maybe it was because we were the oldest, but of all the grandkids, my cousin, Lissa and I devoted more of our summers to learning to ride those little, ornery ponies.

That first summer only Sandy, a chubby, dappled sorrel was big enough to ride. Grandma would lead him around the yard so even the smallest child got to ride. When the novelty for the new ponies lessened with the others, Lissa and I became more determined to train our ponies. They were sweet enough when you had treats for them or brushed the annoying burrs from their shaggy coats. But when a saddle and rider were on their back, they became stubborn and cranky. We were too inexperienced to really know how to make them cooperate. We managed some excitement as a team by taking turns leading each other around on Sandy.

One of our main obstacles was the inseparable bond between the ponies. Sandy would sulk and balk whenever

there was any distance between him and his buddy, Starry, a tiny, bay colt. We discovered, in a desperate sort of way, to use that to our advantage. With Starry locked inside Grandma's milkbarn, we would take turns leading each other away from the barn on Sandy. We would follow the road which circles around the house and then up the hill to the other barn. Sandy, with his rider, was then released. The pony would make a bee-line charge back to his buddy with his rider challenged to stay in the saddle. Together again at the milkbarn, Starry would cease to fret and whinny for Sandy. Switching riders, we would then march back to the other barn and, with a little luck, do it all over again.

Yet somehow, looking back now, with amazement, at just how frenzied some of those trips back to the milkbarn had been, we escaped relatively unscathed. Many of those wild rides back to the milkbarn ended abruptly, prematurely or both. We had horse fever in the worst way and we never stopped trying to become tough little cowgirls. I had a horse now and my determination to master horseback riding had new rewards. On Birdie, I had the freedom to go wherever I wanted. Together we explored the backroads and open fields for miles around.

Each summer for several years after Birdie came to our farm in Central Missouri, we stilled travelled to Grandma and Grandpa's. Birdie had to remain behind. We were allowed to take our smaller, favorite pets for the entire summer. We never had to leave behind our tiny puppies,

Wiggles and Little Bit, the decendents of our family's first Chihuahuas, KayKay and Spunky. Now and then a bunny accompanied us.

For less than one brief year, my favorite pet was a baby goat. Somehow she acquired the name Beaulah. She displayed the distinct visual characteristics of a purebred Nubian goat. She had fawn-like eyes accented by a golden brown mask. In many ways she resembled a black Doberman puppy, but with comical, silver-gray speckled floppy ears. A gray speckled nose and a large white splotch on her forehead completed her endearing apppearance.

Beaulah followed me everywhere with her incessant "baas". Hours and hours were spent together in our playhouse. This 8 foot by 10 foot building had been converted from an old chicken house once used by the original owners of our farm, Luther and Pearl Humbird. The tin-roofed, wooden shed was decorated with miniature children's furniture, curtains, doll houses and toys. Often Beaulah would be dressed in our dolls' clothing.

Beaulah was nearly half-grown the summer Grandpa stopped by enroute for "vacation" from his job in

Kansas City to his farm in the Ozarks. His purpose, his assignment, was to shuttle his 3 grandaughters, now that school was on summer break, to Grandma for the next 3 months. The suitcases along with the 3 young girls and Chihuahuas were loaded into his car. He calmly took in stride the situation when I could not bear to leave Beaulah. Outside the vehicle, Beaulah was baaing, also terribly distressed that she was being left behind. Without hesitation, Grandpa opened a rear-passenger door to his Ford Fairlane to allow the goat to hop in and curl up onto the backseat. As always, Grandma was thrilled to welcome us as we arrived later that evening, baby goat and all.

"Hey Cat" was another cherished pet we insisted join us for her first summer. Her becoming a family member was also memorable. The story goes, as retold many times, the day began with my sister, Jan and cousin, Patty Jean playing under the front porch of Patty Jean's house. We usually called her Patty Jean to differentiate between her and I because we had the same name, Patty.

My aunt and uncle's house was a long trailer set up just outside our front yard, next to the main road. Because of a contentious divorce dispute, Patty Jean and her little sister, Doreen were allowed only to visit their mom on rare occasions. Dorothy, or as we called her, Aunt Dottie, was a new resident to our farm. It was always tragically tearful when the young sisters had to return to their dad and stepmom. Everyone was convinced that their stepmom was a witch. Her mistreatment of the girls, as told by them, made it undeniable. Eventually the courts granted Aunt Dottie custody of the girls to now live with us permanently. By then, they had a little brother, Lawrence Berger III. Everyone called him Larry. Now with a family of 5, my Uncle Sever attached a spacious room to his mobile home to serve as a master bedroom.

But now, finally back to Hey Cat's tale. As the girls were playing, unseen under the porch, a strange car pulled into our driveway. Only stopping briefly, it backed into the road and drove away. A calico kitten was left abandoned in the driveway. The girls went to the kitten, picked it up and chased the car shouting, "Stop! Come back! You lost your cat!".

The car only accellerated down the dusty road and no one ever returned to retrieve their kitten. She remained a member of the family for many years. She had the distinction of being one of the few cats my mom allowed to become a housepet.

Lissa and I would talk for hours of how grand to would be to have a horse. The previous summer her parents had finally agreed to buy her a horse. Lissa insisted I be included in the experience. This was the day she got Babe, a joyous day for her. We were taken to a nearby stockfarm and Lissa was to choose from a small group of horses that fit her riding ability and her parents' budget. She narrowed the field to two horses, a small bay mare and a taller, coffee-gold palamino gelding. After riding each

horse and agonizing over the better qualities, she chose the mare. I would have chosen the palamino. Secretly and desperately, I dreamed of that graceful creature as mine. I always will.

I had been more than a little envious of Lissa until now. Surely she would soon visit. She would then know, firsthand, the reason for my pride and enthusiasm for our new horse.

Chapter 4
A Gift from an Old Cowboy

We could not afford a saddle, so I rode bareback. With Birdie's broad back and slow, steady gaits a saddle was unnecessary. The reach to step into a stirrup would be impossible anyway. The only way to get up on her was to have someone give you a leg-up or find a fence or stump to climb on first.

On our first trip out, Birdie and I turned east onto our country gravel road. My destination was a mile and a half down the road to Beulah and Don Congers' place. They had been neighbors and good friends from the first day we moved to our central Missouri farm. It was late in March, 1963, the year I turned 7. Memories of that spring have hardly faded. Warmer days had nurtured waves of clover and bluegrass into a velvety, emerald carpet in our yard, with borders of sunny, yellow daffodils surrounding our new, but quaint, old farmhouse. Its' spacious porch was shielded from the setting sun with a fragrant clematis vine overtaking a wire trellis. Thousands of tiny white blossoms gave the vine a delicate lacy effect as it billowed up the trellis. This was to be my home for many years to come.

Beulah and Conger, as he was called, instead of Don, had been married more than twenty years. They had become an integral link in our circle of neighbors and friends. In a poignant twist of fate, though they genuinely seemed to adore having children around, were never able to have a child of their own. Even though they were new neighbors, they quickly took on the role of adopted aunt and uncle to my sisters and me. When Mom needed a babysitter, Beulah always insisted on the task. And task, it was, because we were always feisty, into-everything little girls.

BEULAH

Beulah wore her scarlet hair swept up into a bouffant bun, artfully sculpted in hairspray lacquered curls. That image of her always comes to mind first when thinking back of her. Once-a-week appointments to Milady's Beauty Salon and her nightly routine of donning a colorful, flowery nightcap kept every hair in place. She had a jovial and mischievous nature and was adept with pranks on her unsuspecting targets, young and old.

All who knew her also knew of her innermost sorrow to never bear a child. Even I, as a young girl, could see at times, the sadness she tried so hard to mask. Sometimes she would drink to forget. When she was only a little tipsy, she would be in high spirits, silly and giggly. On the rare occasion, when she drank a few too many, she became almost anguished, sobbing over trivial matters. Those were the nights when my mom sometimes answered a late night phone and assured the person on the other end, "Certainly, it was no bother. She would be right there to pick up Beulah and drive her safely home." By the next day, Beulah would again be her usual bubbly, lovable self.

Conger was a calm, steady husband not embarrassed to show fondness to those he cared about, especially Beulah. After 20 years, he frequently said she was "still his girl." This attribute belied his physical appearance. His height was well over six foot. My sisters and I certainly thought he was the tallest man around for miles. Like my dad, when he wasn't farming, he drove a school bus route. He persevered, driving rambunctious country kids, like me, to school far beyond the 20 years required to earn a well-deserved pension when he retired.

Their farm was home to a vast variety of critters. They had nanny goats with tiny, playful kids. Their cantankerous old billy goat, Sam, was notorious for jumping on cars. To protect visitors and their vehicles, Sam was often chained to a tree in the backyard. As all billy goats do, he exuded an offensive, musky odor, making his exile doubly justified. Their menagerie included floppy-eared rabbits, ducks, geese and chickens, even chickens that laid pink, green or blue eggs. They are a true, longstanding breed of domesticated chickens. Originally from South America, they are known as Araucanas.

Conger and several neighborhood buddies spent many nights roaming about through the countryside fox hunting. Foxes were, by now, somewhat rare in the Midwest, so they trained their hounds to track coyote and raccoon as well. From the kennels where he housed his beloved hounds, their bays and incessant howling mingled with the barnyard uproar protesting any visitor's intrusion into their territory.

In his younger days, Conger had, in my opinion, a most exciting career as a ranch hand somewhere in Wyoming. As the saying goes, he was paid for bustin' broncs and wranglin' cattle. Like many ranch hands, he passed his idle time on week-ends competing at rodeos. His last roping horse, Tex, was still alive and well. He was "Out to pasture," so they say, with Conger's herd of cattle for company.

So, of course, Beulah and Conger had to be first on my list to show off our new horse. Their tidy, white farmhouse sat far back from the main road with a meandering lane that split the front pasture into two fields. Barbed wire fencing paralleled the snakelike curves along both sides of the road until it intersected the sturdy, white board fence that marked off their yard.

Tex was first to notice the big black mare as we approached the entrance to their property. He was a tall, rangy, red and white paint horse. He had to be nearly 30 years old now. That's the equivalent to 100 in human years. Raising his head up from grazing, he realized we were actually entering his territory. He mustered enough energy to seem excited as he loped over to the fence to greet us. There's no telling how long it had been since he had seen another horse. The horses' noses touched with a brief sniff of each other. They quickly settled in as if they were old acquaintances.

Taking advantage of the stop, Birdie thrust her head forward, pulling enough rein from my grip to graze. The tallest grass grew along our side of the fence. It was just beyond reach of the enclosed grazing herd and too tempting. She rarely passed up an opportunity to devour any food within her reach.

I indulged her a short while, relinquishing all but the last few precious inches of the reins from my possession. She swayed to and fro beneath me snatching quick bites and then maneuvering the wads of grass around the bit to chew. It would take strength from my entire upper body and both arms to tug her head up from the ground. With a few determined prods to her massive flanks with my heels, I managed to coax her forward. Crunching gravel shifted, then tumbled back to rest into the tiny craters left behind as each great hoof lifted and fell. All the while, some stones shot out in different directions, propelled by the force of her weight crushing the gravel as she shuffled along the road.

Now aware of our presence, the foxhounds initiated the intruder alarm with the barnyard gang joining enthusiastically. The volume only increased as we continued to approach. The commotion always brought the couple outside. A sidewalk led from the doorstep to a gated archway adorned in fragrant, lemon-yellow flowering honeysuckle vine. The draping vines prevented Conger's passing through the archway before first ducking his head down. They joined the two of us in the driveway. From time to time I battled with Birdie. She was restless, sidling ever closer to Beulah's honeysuckle to steal a bite as we chatted awhile about usual topics such as school, weather and how Mom was getting along with her new milk cows.

The cows, several Guernseys were purchased from another close neighbor, the Parrott family. Their legacy was an expansive, long-established dairy and milked Guernsey cattle exclusively. Our new cows had been a costly, but worthwhile investment. One of those cows, a red and white cow named Shorty, was now mother to a set of twin heifers. They were tiny as you will ever see, but thriving. For several days since their birth, Mom had devoted extra time to the threesome. Shorty was a little bewildered of her situation. Mom was insuring their chances of survival.

Conger praised me for being a real cowgirl out riding bareback. The truth was, I explained, Birdie's broad back was ideal. She never really got excited about anything or made any sudden moves. I didn't have a saddle anyway. I thought I heard him say,"Something would just have to be done about that". Before I could be on my way, Beulah made me promise to be extra careful going home and be sure to tell my mom, "Hello".

Tex accompianied us back down the driveway along his side of the fence and we headed east again on the gravel road. He whinnied in protest for being left behind, pacing the fence until we were out of sight.

We hadn't travelled far before encountering a most puzzling scene. The lifeless body of a large oppossom was lying on the road. It must have been hit by a passing car or truck, but I could see no evidence of injury or trauma. I couldn't get off to get a closer look. Out here alone, it would be nearly impossible to get back on my horse. I suppose some might call it morbid curosity, but I wanted to find out what might have happened to this animal. I managed to break off a branch from a nearby tree that was long enough to poke at it. When the prodding got no reaction, I gave up the investigation and continued our ride.

At the first crossroad, I decided to turn back for home. As we approached the exact spot where I had found the dead oppossom less than 30 minutes earlier, it had vanished. No one else had passed by during that time. Had the oppossum, when hearing a large creature approaching, pretended to be dead, then make its' escape later? That day, I believe I discovered, first hand, the origin of the phrase "playing possum".

As we arrived home later that afternoon, we met Mom coming from her garden where she had been weeding. She had been watching for me to get back and was relieved that I had made it home safely. As she would often say, "All in one piece". To this day she worries. In my 50-plus years of horseback riding, I've always had the good fortune, and the constant vigil of my guardian angel to find my way home to ride another day. She wanted me know that Conger had stopped by earlier with a gift. He had left it in the barn.

Instantly curious to find out what his gift was, I dismounted my horse, not an easy feat with the ground so far away. After flopping across her back like a sack of potatoes on your belly, you cling tightly to her mane, then slide towards the ground, feet first. The last few feet to the ground are in freefall as you release your grip on her mane. Now safely back on the ground, I led Birdie through the gate and into her pasture. Struggling with her as she insisted on attacking the grass before even clearing the gate, I slipped the bridle off. With the snaffle bit clinking along the way, I rushed to the barn. What was Conger's gift?

Startled, cackling chickens scattered as I burst through the barn door. Dust and feathers, highlighted in the rays of sunshine sneaking in between boards, swirled and floated downward. At the end of the barn aisle, a saddle sat perched on the front panel of Birdie's stall. Mom entered the barn just behind me. She explained that this saddle had been one of Conger's. He was pretty sure he wouldn't use it again. He wanted me to have it.

The leather was stiff and dusty from years unused in his barn, but I could see beyond the layers of dirt, the inevitable bird droppings and even a few mud dauber nests that time had settled upon the saddle. With a little saddle soap and mink oil, the crackly, faded leather was transformed to a supple, rich chestnut brown. Now the saddle actually showed the promise of a few more good years of service. A well-worn patch remained on the pommel where a lasso had rubbed the leather from roping cattle, a badge attesting its' authenticity as a true cowboy's saddle.

Chapter 5
Saddle Up!

Shortly after getting the saddle, the rare occasion of a visit from Aunt Carolyn and her three children finally happened. They were travelling to Grandma and Grandpa's. To break up the long trip, they stopped at our house for the afternoon before resuming their trip. At last, my cousin, Lissa, the only person I knew at that time as enamored with horses as myself, was going to meet Birdie.

Persuading Aunt Carolyn to allow Lissa and I to ride Birdie that afternoon had been a challenge. We were reminded they still had more than 120 miles to travel that day. After assuring her we would be very careful and not go far, she granted our request and added she hoped we would have a good time. As we escaped towards the barn, we were thankful for the balmy day, perfect for being outdoors. Nothing would have deterred us anyway once we had her permission.

In spite of my explicit description of Birdie, Lissa was not prepared for the giant horse awaiting us in her stall. In amazement, she repeated, again and again, how incredible it was, how lucky I must feel, to have her. "That's incredible" was one of Lissa's favorite phrases. It probably still is. Undaunted by her size, like me, Lissa was completely at ease with Birdie's remarkable, calm nature. Nor was she apprehensive about riding her. If you knew how to read horses, in Birdie's expressions, in her demeanor, she communicated trust and affection.

As we had done so many times before with the ponies, we began our ritual of saddling up. Essentials in our routine were a thorough grooming and an inspection of the mare's feet for hidden stones or other injuries. This assures you the horse is fit, or sound, to ride. Mastering the skill of dislodging mud and rocks from a horse's hooves with a hoof pick requires time, patience, horse-savvy and a cooperative horse. Horses enjoy the the attention, and with a consistant routine they learn to anticipate the process. After a dutiful, soothing grooooming they expect to be ridden.

Between the two of us, we managed to hoist the saddle upon the mare's back. Seeing it on Birdie for the first time, it looked oddly tiny. Struggling to tighten a girth strap with barely enough length to encircle her great chest was not an easy task. Together we found the strength to secure the buckle. Satisfied that our combined effort wouldn't get the girth cinched any tighter, I bridled her and led her from the stall.

It was impossible for me lift my foot high enough to step into the stirrup. Cupping her hands together, Lissa assisted me into the saddle. She then climbed upon the loading chute at the edge of the corral and waited for me to circle Birdie around. I reined the horse alongside Lissa's perch. In a quick, practiced motion, before Birdie could sidle away, she stepped into the stirrup and hopped on behind.

With the task of saddling up out of the way and our good fortune to be firmly planted high up in the saddle, I urged Birdie into a trot. We exited the driveway and turned left onto the road. A short way beyond to our right begins a neighbor's open hay field. In other words, no fence surrounded the field, allowing us to move off the rocky road to ride through the tall grass along the edge of the field.

Just ahead, the terrain slopes upward. Encouraging our horse into a faster pace, she lumbered forward with her ears cocked forward in a casual, relaxed manner. Birdie's head rose up and forward each time she gathered herself beneath us. Her thick and unruly mane tossed in rhythm with the drumming of her hooves on the ground. On a leisurely, galloping horse, the affect over its' rider is mesmerizing. In that moment, the melding of a willing, cheerful horse and its' rider can be unmistakably therapeutic.

But in a split second, without a vigilant instinct

for the unexpected, an unforeseen disaster sometimes unfolds before you. My recollection of the events during the next few seconds always replays as surreal and in slow motion. The saddle began slipping. Lissa was clinging to me steadfastly. We remained in the mutinous saddle. It rotated from a terrifying, sideways position aligning us parallel to the ground, to slipping completely under the horse's belly. Not until our abrupt impact with the ground, did we cease our panicked commands of "Whoa, Birdie!"

Dazed, but unharmed, lying flat on our backs, our view was Birdie's shaggy underbelly directly above. She had stopped, dead in her tracks, the instant we hit the ground! She remained calm and still while we scrambled to our feet and not under hers. I have no doubt Birdie stopped to protect us from being trampled. Was this one of countless times my guardian angel intervened? Regardless of whether she was obeying her heart, or obeying an angel, Birdie was a most extraordinary creature!

In determined cowgirl fashion, we repositioned the troublesome saddle and mustered every ounce of our strength to tighten the girth enough to hold the saddle secure for the remainder of our ride. For the second time I stepped into Lissa's cupped hands and mounted our horse. Our dilemma for getting Lissa aboard was solved by easing Birdie into the ditch between the road and the field. From the high side of the ditch, she was able to slide into her seat behind me. Having no desire to relive the previous scene, we continued our ride at a slower, cautionary pace. It was many years later before I commonly used a saddle again.

From the front porch, our mothers had witnessed everything. Yet upon our safe return later that afternoon, no hysteria resulting from the event was evident. They must have known the futility of forbidding us to ever ride horses again. Maybe they truly believed in our ability to handle the situation. More than likely, it was a combination of both. I am grateful to have been a recipient of that faith and support.

Chapter 6
The More, the Merrier

Growing up in the country, in the early 1960's, meant finding unique ways to entertain ourselves. There were no malls or arcades nearby, no playgrounds, only our imagination to create playhouses from old sheds in the barnyard or mazes through the bales of hay, high up in the vast barnloft. One rainy afternoon, we spent the most delightful time mudsliding downhill along a well-worn cowpath.

There were 8 of us in our exclusive, little country-bumpkin neighborhood gang. Exclusive meant, in our rural area, there were no other girls our age for miles around. All girls, of course, as we were not yet fond of boys. There was myself, my younger sisters, Deb and Jan, our cousins, Patty Jean and Doreen, and neighbors, Connie, Pam and Kathleen. Once, 3 brothers whose family had recently moved nearby, wandered, uninvited, into our playday. Reluctantly, we allowed them to join in, only to end the morning chucking gravel at them in the middle of the road to send them home. In later years, they continued to be hoodlums prowling the countryside at night smashing mailboxes and stealing gas from their neighbors' tractors.

Patty Jean and Doreen had silky blonde hair and the biggest, sweetest blue eyes. At the ages of 5 and 3, we adopted them as our cousins when their mother married my uncle. The family lived with us on the farm for several years. To this day they are endearing members of our family. Adjusting to rural life, at times, wasn't easy for them. Imagine younger versions of Paris Hilton and Nicole Richie in their television sitcom, "The Simple Life", minus the million dollar lifestyle, of course. Drama and "dumb, blond moments" were our reality. Eventually, we converted them into tomboys like the rest of us.

Connie and Pam had always lived on a farm nearby. A ten-minute walk across cow pastures and hayfields separating our house from theirs. The sisters resembled Barbie dolls with their tall slender builds, lovely looks and perfect pixie haircuts. Their father had 3 brothers, each with farms and families nearby. With so many cousins and kin around, regrettably, they couldn't come to play often. On those fortunate, rare occasions, they were always truly fearless alongside us in our adventures. Their gregarious, self-confident nature was a trait common throughout their family.

In the opposite direction and about the same distance

away, was Kathleen's home. Kathleen was a big-boned girl with a sweet smile and a gentle naivety. Her long, golden brown hair was always in braids. Her family belonged to the Mennonite community.

Their simplistic church was less than 3 miles from our home with an abundant number in the congregation. Many lived within close proximity of the church. Their presense added yet another layer of diversity and culture to our community, a community set apart from most small towns. This religous sect went by the name, "Dunkards" because of their firm belief in baptism for all members of their church. Strict dress codes are required for their members. Women and girls were to wear plain dresses, aprons, stockings and delicate net bonnets to demonstrate modesty. Men were attired in traditional Amish work garments and remained unshaven after they wed..Use of electricity and many modern conveniences were banned by the church as prideful luxuries.

Keeping up with tomboy friends was difficult and uncomfortable in her proper attire. When Kathleen came to play, we would provide shorts and a tee-shirt for her to wear. At the end of the day she would change back into her dress before returning home. Because she feared her family might not approve of this casual, borrowed clothing, it always remained our secret. The justification, we felt, was worthy as Kathleen delighted in those times when she could be carefree for a while.

Some days were spent fishing down at the creek that

crossed through our land. To fish, you need bait. As youngsters, almost stranded in the country, you must be resourceful. We had to consider options available to us within our immediate surroundings. Digging earthworms in the manure-rich barnlot was one. Other options were chasing and catching spring-loaded, elusive grasshoppers before they could hide in the grassy fields or searching out fat crickets scurrying about the damp, dark wellhouse floor. You must learn to secure a grasshopper with a quick pinch to their back or wings before they can bite you (It hurts.) or spit their nasty "tobacco juice" all over your hands. It also takes teamwork to place the newly-caught insects into a jar and not let any already in the jar escape.

These are examples of the extremes we would take in finding our bait. For a short time, each summer, the best bait, by far, is horseflies. Not the easiest to catch, but Birdie and a few of the savvy, gentler milkcows, battle-weary from the flies' onslaught, were tolerant of us jumping and snatching at the persistant, buzzing flies. Our capture of the flies granted them some relief from their tormentors' vicious bites.

We fashioned fishing poles from saplings and string. When fishing hooks were scarce, we used safety pins. Believe it or not, you can catch a fish with a safety pin, though it is more of a a challenge. Oh sure, the objective was to be the one who landed the biggest, or the most fish. The truth was tiny sun perch were the only fish, besides minnows, to be found in those shallow pools.

In essence, time idly spent under one particular giant Sycamore tree, utterly dwarfed by it and cloaked within the cool of its' deep abundant shade was always blissful. Its' tangle of massive roots, exposed by flooding water, reached out beyond the creekbank, arching to and fro, over our fishing hole. Climbing out amongst them you could find the ideal lounge, lie back in it and relax. My childhood memories would not be complete without recalling the carefree hours, tranquility and majesty that tree provided.

One partiularly close friend must be included in this childhood horse tale. Although not within walking distance to join in with my near-by gang of eight, we shared joyous, sometimes daring, adventures.

Ater my family's move to the country, Julie and I immediately became friends while riding the same bus to school everyday, Throughout our 12 year school career, it had always been Bus #6. The seat beside us was always reserved for the other. The exception to this was those times when one or the other, though rarely, became too rambunctious. As punishment, the offender was forced to sit in the front seat alone behind our bus driver, Otis. One time,in particular, I remember getting into trouble was for annoyingly snapping Julie's elastic garter straps.

Long, bouncing, golden curls, sparkling blue eyes and her soft-spoken, lady-like manners defied the fact that Julie was also a tough, little cowgirl. Her riding abilities were far beyond mine during our first years together. Of course I admired and envied her for so many reasons.

In addition to raising hogs and cattle, Julie's family farm had a small herd of Shetland ponies. The abundant variety, in color and size, of mares, their sassy stallion and tiny, foals roaming the fields surrounding their house intrigued me.

Peanut, small, but plucky, was their most well-behaved pony. A cup of hot cocoa with melted marshmallows floating on top may best describe his chocolate-brown, bold dappled coat. I was allowed to ride Peanut on those rapturing occasions when I would visit their home while Julie rode one of the other livelier ponies. In a few, short years, we outgrew Peanut as our longer legs inched closer to the ground.

Often our time together included two other children uniquely related to Julie. Mikey and Glenda were brother and sister but they were also Julie's nephew and niece, yet there was very little age difference betwen the four of us. Julie was the youngest of three siblings, but her older sister and brother were grown and maried before she was born. We share so many grand memories, on Mikey and Glenda's grandparent's farm, of horseback riding, fishing and swimming at their spectacular lake secluded more than a mile away on a back corner of the property.

Julie's parents, Ruth and Norval were quite devout. Her father was a deacon. It was a given, when I was their guest, we attended church on Sunday and the first week of each summer the entire neighborhood gathered for vacation bible school at the nearby Mt. Zion Baptist Church. I was truly an honorary family member of their warm, generous group.

Julie was adopted into my family, as well. Sisterhood entitled her to experience, first hand, extended summer stays in the Ozarks as a welcomed, extra grandchild.

In return, the next summer, I travelled with Julie's family to Memphis, Tennessee. Memphis was home for Mike and Glenda. I loved sight seeing for my first time in a big, southern city. As a young teen, our stop at Graceland, Elvis Presley's mansion, was a wondrous, once in a life time, experience for me. For a memento, I plucked a cluster of prickly, green leaves from a holly bush just outside the mansion's distinctly embellished wrought iron entrance gate. The wrought iron musical notes throughout the fence, mimicing sheets of music, were unforgettable, as were the holly leaves tucked away in a keepsake box.

Wintertime at the farm could be extreme. Many times snowfall totals resulted in school closings for extended periods. It was always a joyous day for us when the school bus did not arrive at its' appointed time. On those snowy days, we always bundled ourselves in layers of winter clothing to play in the snow. Powerful northern winds commonly formed dunes of snow, building sometimes to heights of 5 or 6 feet. The tallest drifts could always be found along our road where high roadbanks and fences trapped the blowing snow. We would carve caves or igloos from the embankments. Several trips would have to be made back to the farmhouse for changes into dry winter gear. Often we had to resort to substituting our dad's cotton socks for gloves when every pair of gloves available were too soaked to keep our hands warm.

On one early Christmas at the farm, my sisters and I received a toboggan as a gift. We anxiously awaited the next heavy snowfall. When that day finally arrived, it unfolded into a rodeo, not a typical day of sledding.

Our farm consisted of rolling hills that were not ideal for exhilarating downhill sledding. Someone pushing or pulling the toboggan by it's rope was the extent of our forward motion down the hill. In a short time, we were exhausted in our efforts to make our day of sledding a thrilling event. I was struck with a better plan.

Nearby, in the same pasture where we were playing, several of our cattle were also trudging through the snow. Gentle, older Jill was among them. She had been moved from my grandparent's farm to ours with three others when we bought our farm. These cows represented the formation of my mom's first herd. With a tiny trailer, borrowed from Conger, she had moved them here one by one.

My rationale seemed simple. Jill was still a pet in our family. Although Jill was older now, she would still tolerate children climbing aboard for cow rides. We added a longer rope to our toboggan as a harness to loop around Jill's neck. She would become our sleigh "horse."

The perfect solution, don't you think?

After harnessing the toboggan to the cow, we did not even have time to get positioned on the sled. Spooked by the contraption behind, she bolted. I can't tell you how long we chased and cajoled her through the snow to retrieve our toboggan. When we and our togoggan finally returned home, no one mentioned Jill's participation in our tobogganing adventure.

JILL + OUR TOBOGGAN

It was many years later before we revealed those details to our mom. As always, she was only vaguely surprised.

Those hottest of summer days were meant for swimming. The best place to swim was farther upstream on our neighbor's adjoining farmland, too far upstream to travel by foot. Treks of longer distances took on a different perspective with our group because of our age differences. At times, the younger girls, especially Doreen, would tire. Though we likely threatened them, we couldn't leave them behind in the woods, alone and exhausted. On those occasions, the older girls would share the responsiblity of toting them piggy-back to finish the journey. Birdie became our solution for getting everyone easily to our favorite swimming hole so far away.

Row after row of corn, wheat, oats or soybeans, flowed in waves with the summer breeze up and over the rolling hill, parallelling the dirt road heading east past our home. This was our neighbor's adjoining field, and through it, the best route to to our secluded country pool. At the southern boundary of the crop field, the original, untouched woodlands surrounding the creek basin remain. Once in the woods, the sloping terrain hastens your pace on the path downward to the creek below. The bluffs, steep inclines and flood plains, maybe totalling 100 acres, were always a perfect site for adventure. This scenic, pristine landscape was our natural waterpark.

At the heart of these ancient, flowing waters, their course sharply diverted into a snake-like bow in the creek's meandering journey through the hillsides. Eternity had sculpted rock bluff embankments towering above a deep, chilly, indigo-blue pool carved from its' base. This legendary arena we had discovered enchanted all within it. Dependent on the area's resourses and natural shelter, Native Americans, mainly the Osage had camp settlements on this very bank long, long ago. Native artifacts, most commonly arrowheads, could be found along the creekbed.

After heavy rains, the rising waters churn the sand and stone creekbed exposing arrowheads, hidden for centuries, on the banks and sandbars as the water levels recede. These were the ideal times to search for arrowheads. In our family, hunting arrowheads rose to the level of competitive sport, with Mom and Dad frequently joining the hunt. With eyes sweeping back and forth along the creekbed, you try to discern the distinctive, chiseled flint arrowheads. They are deftly camouflaged among the endless creekstone and sand tumbled into mesmerizing waves of sandbars flowing downstream alongside

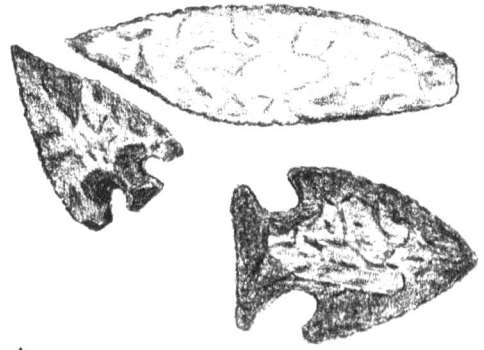

ARROWHEADS

the lively water. Each hunter's goal was to discover the greatest number of arrowheads or at least the most skillfully crafted relic at each outing.

Once, as I hunted arrowheads alone, fate again smiled on me as I learned another important lesson in how snap decisions can put you in danger. While travelling upstream, I encountered a large, deep pool of water. To by-pass the pool and continue hunting upstream, I climbed up and out of the creekbed. At the top of the bank, through the tall reeds, a tiny, pink piglet appeared. Then, another.

They were far too irresistably cute and vulnerable alone in these woods. Thinking I was rescuing them from any predators that might find them, I snagged the first one by a hind leg. The piglet began struggling and squealing. As I tucked it under my arm and set out to capture the second one, I heard the angry grunts of a large sow and the crackling, swishing and snapping of branches as she crashed through the underbrush towards me. It took only a split second to realize these piglets were not orphans and I had made their mama extremely mad!

Dropping my good intentions, in terror, I ran 50 yards or so through the woods, with the enraged sow relentlessly pursuing. I knew I was running for my life, surely screaming hysterically. Still ahead of the sow, I reached the fence dividing the woods from our pasture. Squirming through the gap between the top, single strand of barbed wire and the woven wire, I tumbled to the ground. Inches separated me from the enormous, hell-bent sow held back by the wire mesh barrier.

The sow's fury was justified towards me. She was only protecting her piglets. If the distance to the fence had been farther, or I had stumbled, I would not have escaped. Once again, I felt thankful for my ever-vigilant angel.

On the days we planned to swim, we would meet at my house. Kathleen would change from her dress to a borrowed swimsuit. With Birdie bridled, we would draw straws. Birdie's ample, broad bareback could accomodate everyone. The purpose of drawing straws was to determine who was not riding horseback to the swimming hole. After assisting everyone else atop the towering draft mare, stranded below, the person who drew the short straw had to walk. On the bright side, she was guaranteed a seat on the ride home. Whoever drew the short straw at the creek at the end of the day walked home.

Splashing and playing in the sparkling cool water on

those hot summer days was our perfect way to beat the heat. We would spend time exploring the shoreline for musselshells or arrowheads. We would try to decypher the animal tracks in the mud and sandbars to discover what wildlife had ventured through. I can remember channelling schools of tiny fish into shallow inlet pools. I marvelled at the brilliant, shimmering, colorful fish, so abundant in the fresh water. It was like chasing rainbows.

Although we were enjoying our afternoon, Birdie had to impatiently wait the time tied to a tree at the bank. Swarms of deerflies and mosquitoes, spawned from the outer pools, incessantly harrassed her. Throughout the day, in rotation, someone was posted beside her to swat at any of her tormentors that were beyond her swishing tail. A few of us were capable of walking her along the bank to graze without letting her escape. Once, while grazing, she pulled the reins away from one of the younger girls. Realizing she was free, she jerked her head high and with a triumphant snort, bolted home. Everyone drew the short straw that afternoon.

Unlike Birdie, we were always reluctant to leave. After coaxing any wading stragglers out of the creek, the next challenge was boosting all aboard the fidgeting mare. In a chaotic battle of wills, Birdie, anxious to leave, tossed her head and side-stepped as, one by one, her passengers struggled up and on. Like most horses, the urgency to get home quickened her pace. Her uncharacteristic rambunctious burst of energy always thrilled her riders.

Clinging, as one, upon this nearly 1-ton living, breathing, gentle giant, the day's unforgettable journey ends, home once again.

As much as I cherished Birdie, there came a time when I knew I had outgrown her. Not in size, of course, but in my riding abilities. I wanted the challenge of riding a fast horse, a horse that loved barrel racing, cutting cows and climbing the steep trails winding through the rugged terrain of our nearby nature park. Older now, I was working week-ends and summers. With the income I saved, I bought my next horse.

Finally, Birdie had earned her leisure days ahead. After several years with little girls instead of plows and heavy loads, she was now fully retired. My experiences with Birdie strengthened my confidence to step up to the next level in horseback riding. Mutual trust is the key to a successful relationship between a horse and rider. Although Birdie had the size and power advantage over me, she never betrayed that trust or intentionally harmed me. There is no doubt. Birdie was a great, big horse with an even bigger heart.

www.ingramcontent.com/pod-product-compliance
Lightning Source LLC
Chambersburg PA
CBHW060816270326
41930CB00002B/54